One-Minute
INSPIRATIONS
for *Women*

ELIZABETH GEORGE

HARVEST HOUSE PUBLISHERS
EUGENE, OREGON

Cover by Harvest House Publishers, Inc., Eugene, Oregon

Adapted from *A Woman After God's Own Heart ® —A Daily Devotional*

ONE-MINUTE INSPIRATIONS FOR WOMEN
Copyright © 2013 by Elizabeth George
Published by Harvest House Publishers
Eugene, Oregon 97402
www.harvesthousepublishers.com

ISBN 978-0-7369-5740-3 (pbk.)
ISBN 978-0-7369-5741-0 (eBook)

Printed in the United States of America

16 17 18 19 20 21 / BP-SK / 10 9

A Note from Elizabeth

Imagine placing God foremost in your heart each morning and striking out on His path for your day, deliberately living for Him. As you commit yourself to God each day, He will work in your heart!

I pray these devotions for busy women like you will help inspire you to draw nearer to God and live out His plans for you. How is this done? The answer: via small steps with big results—living God's way... one day at a time. Practicing God's order of priorities for you...one day at a time. Committing the many different areas of your life to God...one day at a time.

Treat yourself to jewels of wisdom based on God's Word each day. Enjoy the scriptures and messages in this devotional created just for you, a woman who loves the Lord with all her heart. Be inspired to grow. Be willing to change. Be encouraged to take bold steps in handling your problems or facing difficulties. Most of all, become more knowledgeable of God's character and His great love for you.

May your journey to greater faith and trust in God be filled with joy and delight!

Elizabeth George

1

God's Grace

❧

Do you know that the sustaining power of God is packaged in His grace? Life can deliver some tough blows, but God's marvelous grace enables us to go from strength to strength through all the trials. Second Corinthians 12:9 promises that God's grace is sufficient—that it is made perfect in our weakness. I know that encourages my heart. Take that trial you're experiencing and bring it to the Lord. Lay it at His feet. Look to Him. Count on His grace and power in every situation. It's there. It's given to you. And it brings the peace you so long for.

Bless you in your journey to become a woman after God's own heart.

Father, my heart overflows with the love and blessings You've given me. Even in the midst of my trials and sorrow I can be joyful in my heart because I know You are in charge. Amen.

2

The Things of God

❧

Redeeming your time is so important. What do I mean? Time is redeemed when you make the most of your life by fulfilling God's purposes. As you line up your life and seize every opportunity for useful service, your life takes on an efficient quality. That may be difficult to imagine since you're so busy, but as you focus on doing the business of God, time expands. I don't know who wrote this poem, but it's so true:

I have only just a minute.
Only sixty seconds in it…
Just a tiny little minute.
But eternity is in it.

As your heart becomes more dedicated to God, you'll reclaim, recover, retrieve, rescue, and regain the minutes, hours, and days of your life for His glory.

Jesus, what a precious gift time is! Please keep me aware of my stewardship of this great award. Help me make good use of every hour, realizing that once spent, it can never be returned to me. Amen.

Guard Your Time

❀

What stole your day from you today? Was it putting off something you knew you should do? Something important for living out God's plan for your life? It's been said, "If you don't plan your day, someone else will plan it for you." Who's the best person to create your schedule? You, of course! Who has prayed through your priorities and desires to do God's will? It's you again, dear friend. Don't let someone plan your day who is clueless about your goals and your God-given desires and priorities. God has given you today to serve Him. Plan your day. Schedule your day. Protect your day.

Lord, surely You have set the hours of my day before me. Help me guard them diligently, making the most of each moment. Give me wisdom as I plan the many details of my busy life. Most of all, keep me mindful of You in the midst of everything I have to do. Amen.

A "Today" Resolution

❧

You don't have to wait until New Year's Day to make a resolution about your schedule. Why not make one today? First, pray over your priorities: "Lord, what is Your will for me at this time of my life?" Now plan through your priorities and prepare a schedule: "Lord, when should I do the things that live out these priorities today?" Ask the Lord to give you direction for your day: "Lord, I only have a limited time left in my day. What do I need to focus on?" Prepare for tomorrow: "Lord, how can I better live out Your plan for my life?" Let the Lord know you appreciate Him: "Lord, thank You for this day…and the opportunity to talk with You directly." Then go forth with confidence and joy.

Lord, my life is Yours. I want to please You in everything I do. I need Your guidance and strength and stamina. I love You. Amen.

5

A Present for You

❧

I want to give you two presents right now: the gift of encouragement…and applause for a job well done in caring for your home. As one person put it, "The greatest priority in a home should be love. If a wife loves her husband and her children, she is well on the way to making the marriage and the home a success." Proverbs 9:1 says, "Wisdom has built her house, she has hewn out her seven pillars." It took me a while to discover there's no greater task, responsibility, and privilege in this world than to make a house a home. I know that takes work, which is not always appreciated. I truly honor what it takes to be a woman, a wife, and a mother today. Thank you for all you do to take care of yourself and your family. I pray that God will continue to bless you richly.

Lord, I thank You for the house I call home. Give me insight and wisdom in making my home reflect Your presence. You are welcome here! Amen.

6

A Special Time

❧

Why not plan a special night for your family? If you're not married, get friends together. Give everyone plenty of notice, especially if teens are involved. When the time comes around, prepare a festive meal, go out to dinner, or order pizza!

Later, gather around and have everyone share what they've done in the past three months that was fun and meaningful. Encourage each person to share a goal or dream…and be supportive. Dreams aren't always based on current reality. Talk about the childhood antics of the kids, how you and your husband grew up, what your parents did, where your grandparents lived. Share your faith experiences…and let others share theirs. End your time together by drawing people's names out of a hat and committing to doing two nice things for that person during the week.

Lord, You've given me a wonderful family and awesome friends. I delight in being with these people You've given me to cherish…and I especially delight in You. Amen.

No More Gossip

❀

"No more gossip." What an admirable goal! One of the most common questions I get from women centers around gossiping: "How can I avoid sharing it and listening to it?" Philippians 4:8 says, "Whatever things are true…noble…just…pure…meditate on these things." In other words think godly thoughts about others. And if any of your thoughts about others don't measure up to God's guidelines, they're out! Confess them, deal with them, and be done with them. A powerful truth is that if we love the Lord, love His Word, love His people, and love one another, we won't want to gossip. It's that simple…and that important.

Lord, You hate gossip! You abhor words that diminish another person. Help me look at others through Your eyes and think only the best about them, especially when awkward situations arise. I don't want others to gossip about me, so I choose not to gossip about them. Amen.

8

Love Is a Decision

❧

Loving your husband is a daily choice. Love may start out as a good feeling, but to love someone long-term is an act of the will. It means loving someone even when he may not be lovable at that particular moment. Hopefully your husband is your best friend. Enjoy being with him. Spoil him. Think about him. Pray for him. Encourage him.

But what if you don't feel this way? The question remains, "Will you love your husband?" Do everything you can—starting right now—to restore your love. Pray for him. Do little acts of kindness for him. Express your love in every way you can. Thoughtful deeds and kind thoughts will reenergize your love and revitalize your marriage. Love is blossoming in you, my friend.

Lord, loving another person can sometimes be trying. But by Your grace I can love my spouse completely. I choose to honor and serve this man I call husband. Help me be the wife he needs. Work in his life so he will be all You envisioned. Amen.

Your Attitudes and Actions

❀

Family is the best place to teach young men and women about God's kind of love. Today let's focus on your daughters. Titus 2, verses 3 through 5, says we're to teach our daughters, our granddaughters, and our younger sisters in Christ the good things in the Christian life, including how to love a husband. What are you modeling in your marriage? Don't be afraid to be affectionate in front of your kids. Let them see and hear that you love your husband. Compliment your spouse and let your kids know you trust and respect him. Don't disparage or nag him. Deal with disagreements privately. Show your children that making sacrifices for another person isn't drudgery. Share scriptures that encourage you and help you live out God's calling as a woman, a wife, a mother.

Lord, marriage is a model of Your love for Your church. May my marriage be representative of that same sacrificial love You have for us. May my family reflect Your values and priorities. And may others see in us the beauty of Christian love. Amen.

10

The Hardest Work

✤

Raising kids can be an uphill battle. I know that from experience! Although we love them dearly, they aren't always the little angels we wish they'd be. When we don't feel very loving does that mean we're being bad mothers? No! We're human...and God knows that. A godly mother loves God with all her heart, soul, mind, and strength. And she passionately and consistently teaches her children to do the same. No one has more potential for godly influence on your children than you and your husband. Pray every day for these little ones and pour God's Word into their lives. Ask God to give you wisdom as you show your kids you love them. Amid the joy of raising children will be some of the hardest life work you'll ever do. And it's one of God's highest callings. Hang in there!

Father, I need Your strength, grace, and mercy as I deal with my kids today. I want to shower them with unconditional love and support. And I want to open their minds and hearts to You. Amen.

The Beginning of Wisdom

❧

Doesn't being a "wise woman" sound like the person is ancient? And we're definitely not there yet! Well, wisdom doesn't necessarily have a thing to do with age. I pray every day for wisdom in my life. I want a life characterized by peace and joy, by order and meaning. Does this sound too good to be true? There's no getting around the fact that a godly life is lived one minute at a time, one thought at a time, one decision at a time. Proverbs 9:10 says, "The fear of the LORD is the beginning of wisdom, and the knowledge of the Holy One is understanding."

My friend if you have a heart for God, read His Word. God is knowledge and God is wisdom. Live according to His high calling.

Father, You are the source of all wisdom. Whenever I am faced with a choice, a decision, a responsibility, may I look to You and Your Word for guidance. Amen.

12

Thou Shalt Be Organized

❧

Are you continually looking for your car keys? Have you misplaced your glasses, the remote control, important paperwork again? How much of your day is spent searching for lost items? Careful planning eliminates a lot of stress. So plan ahead as much as possible. Set aside special places for your things. Hang your keys on a special hook (but not by the door!). Create a decorative box for the remote. Get a monthly bill-paying system up and running. As I've shared before, I work off a list I carry with me. And no, not everything gets done, but more gets done than if I didn't have a list!

Organization is more than just physical. Give careful thought to your schedule so you have time for spontaneity. Allow time for God to take you in a new direction or show you someone in need.

There are few feelings better than being organized. Take the plunge!

Lord, I'm constantly wasting time looking for things. By being organized I'll have more time for the work You have for me. I'll start on it today! Amen.

13

How's Your Attitude?

❧

As you rush to and fro running errands, picking up the kids, getting to work, buying groceries...do you keep a positive attitude? Or do frustration and irritation take over? When I'm frazzled I tend to let go. Losing my temper comes very easily to me, along with the desire—and sometimes the action!—to tell someone exactly how I feel and what I think. But I want to practice what I preach. And believe me, it sometimes takes all of God's strength in my life to help me do... nothing! To not react. I continually ask God to fill me with His love and patience, two key elements the Bible calls fruit of the Spirit (Galatians 5:22). We're called on to exhibit the same loving patience Jesus had. And how busy we are doesn't fit into the equation.

Lord, when things don't go the way I planned or something interferes with my plans I get so frustrated. Help me be more flexible. And give me the wisdom and grace to respond in love to the people involved. Amen.

Joy and Rejoicing

❧

"Is this it? Is this all there is to life? When does the fun start?" Do you feel this way? My friend, God's Word can cheer you like nothing else. The prophet Jeremiah reported, "Your words, oh God, were found…and Your word was to me the joy and rejoicing of my heart" (Jeremiah 15:16). Rush to the Word of the Lord. God's peace and perspective are available to you now even when grief and gloom are part of your day. The Bible will teach you, correct you, instruct you, guide you, and, yes, cheer you up and give you hope. Make the heart of your life for God a passion for His Word. Spend your time learning about Jesus. This is what you need for your life journey!

Lord, I'm bogged down. My days seem dreary and mundane. I'm going to read Your Word today. Open my mind and heart to Your wisdom, Your love, and Your purpose for my life. Thank You. Amen.

A Unique Boundary

❉

We all need to take time for ourselves, time to revitalize, reenergize, recoup, and refresh. But may I suggest a unique boundary? A dear friend of mine—a brave one, I might add—shared her discipline in the Word. Donna doesn't allow herself to spend more time in any personal activity each day than she spends in the Word of God. She passed this principle on to me, and I've made it part of my life too. A word of warning! If you get serious about establishing this practice, your life, your priorities, your schedule, and your interests are going to change.

Is that the ground I hear rumbling?

Lord, in my heart I want to make You my first priority, but I don't always follow through when it comes to my thoughts and actions. Help me to guard my time with You more jealously. Amen.

Pray, My Friend

❧

"I'd pray more often, but I run out of stuff to say." I can certainly relate. To grow in the Lord, the reading and studying of God's Word is essential. And so is prayer. In fact, prayer is one of the privileges we have as Christians.

The Bible calls us to a life of faithful prayer, which isn't always easy. One of the best incentives to pray is that it strengthens us and short-circuits our tendency to sin. Prayer also gives us the strength and wisdom to follow through on the teachings in the Bible.

If prayer is difficult for you, set aside a small amount of time for prayer every day. Gradually increase that time as you settle into this routine. And you can talk to God about anything. No question, no problem, no concern is too big or too small for Him to handle!

Lord, calm my spirit as I come to You with praise and share my concerns. Give me the courage to talk to You and the patience to listen for Your response. Amen.

17

Be Careful Little Mind

※

Are you dreaming of an ice cream sundae? Or maybe yearning for designer jeans? Perhaps you're tempted by forbidden fruit? Ah, dear friend, you have control over what you think—and you must engage this power! What exactly does this mean? Answer: Disciplining those thoughts of yours. There's a nursery song my kids used to sing: "Be careful little mind what you think." That says it all! You've got to be careful and guard your mind against thoughts that might lead you down sin's path. "Sow a thought, reap an action" is sage advice. Our actions, habits, character, and future are definitely affected by our thoughts. Colossians 3:1 and 2 says to "seek those things which are above" and to "set your mind on those things above, not on things on the earth." Aim your thoughts higher and higher. And "be careful little mind what you think."

My thoughts go astray often, Lord. Sometimes I'm not even sure where these questionable thoughts come from! Help me meditate on Your love and the tremendous joy following Your precepts gives me. Amen.

18

Spiritual Nip and Tuck

❋

I've come to the point in my spiritual growth that I believe strongly that if my physical life is important to God, it should also be important to me. But how far should I take this? What are good guidelines? Makeover TV shows and the widespread use of cosmetic surgery exploit the attitude that "this is my body, and I can do with it as I please." But this couldn't be more wrong! God owns our bodies. They're not ours. The body of a believer is to be used for God's glory. The way we talk and our behavior should reflect positively on Him (1 Corinthians 6:20).

Face lifts and such aren't specifically banned, but make sure vanity and pride aren't the roots of your desire. Concentrate on becoming physically fit and active. Find something you can do with your husband, your kids, or your friends. And while you're out there exercising, keep your eyes and ears open for opportunities to share your faith in Jesus!

Jesus, make me over in Your image. I want to become more like You every day. In everything I do I want to honor You. Amen.

Heaven on Earth

Would you describe what goes on in your home as "heaven on earth"? That's quite an expression, isn't it? Heaven on earth! Do you know that your home life is meant to be exactly that? The Bible uses home life and marriage as illustrations of God's relationship with His church, with the people who choose to follow Him. And when you live out your God-ordained roles and fulfill your God-given assignments others take notice and see proof of our special relationship with the Lord.

You have the privilege of presenting a picture of what heaven will be like to those around you. When you pursue with passion and purpose God's design for a woman, a homemaker, a wife, a mother, you establish a home that reflects the order and beauty of life in heaven. An amazing opportunity, isn't it?

I'm only human, Lord. How can I have a home and marriage that reflects Your perfect love, Your perfect peace? I want to grow in these areas. I want to point people to You. Amen.

All Things Are New

❀

Before I accepted Christ I did my own thing. I did what I wanted and chased after my goals. And my marriage and family suffered. By God's grace I accepted Christ in my late twenties—and it saved my marriage. Second Corinthians 5:17 says, "If anyone is in Christ, [she] is a new creation; old things have passed away—all things have become new." Suddenly for the first time in my life I had something in my life to empower me. I felt worthwhile and truly alive. I earnestly started seeking God's will for my life. Through His Word I'm discovering more and more about what it means to be a woman after God's own heart. As I share that knowledge with you and we grow in the Lord together, I hope you're encouraged to study the Bible on your own too.

Heavenly Father, thank You for my salvation and my new life in Christ. Every day I want to learn more about You so I can live according to Your plan and share Your great love with others. Amen.

"I Do!"

Is your marriage growing a bit stale? Are you stuck in a marriage rut? This might be a good time to think back and recall why you said "I do" in the first place. Remember those crazy things you did when you were dating? The laughter? The fun? The way to recapture those happier days is by making sure each day involves the same lighthearted joy. Proverbs 5:18 says a husband and wife are to continually rejoice in one another.

Here are a few tips to help in that direction. They're right out of Scripture, so we know they'll work! Sprinkled through the book of Proverbs are these caveats: don't be contentious, don't nag, and don't embarrass your husband by your speech, your appearance, or your behavior. Are you wondering what your husband's responsibilities are? That's between him and God. Right now God wants you to concentrate on you!

Dear Jesus, give me guidance in ways I can keep my marriage healthy...and growing...and loving...and fun. I also want it to be centered on You. Amen.

Humble Yourself

❧

English preacher Charles Haddon Spurgeon said, "Humility is the proper estimate of oneself." Humility begins when we know ourselves. Yes, we're made in the image of God, but Romans 3:23 reminds us, "For all have sinned and fall short of the glory of God." Romans 12:2 tells us, "Do not be conformed to this world, but be transformed by the renewing of your mind, that you may prove what is that good and acceptable and perfect will of God." This renewing is done through faithful praying, when we bow before God, confessing our sins, thanking and praising Him for all He's done for us. And then we can strive to imitate Christ's humbleness. And humility also includes respecting others by serving them and considering them better than ourselves. It's a tall order, but we can do all things through Christ!

Father, I don't like to think of myself as selfish or better than others, but sometimes what I do communicates that. Help me focus on You so I can present You to others without me getting in the way. Amen.

That One Thing

❧

You may have heard the expression, "But one thing I do…" What is that "one thing" in your life? In Philippians 3:13-14 the apostle Paul said his "one thing" was to forget what is behind and reach forward to what's ahead, pressing on toward the goal to win the prize of the upward call of God in Christ Jesus. I encourage you to be like a runner—never looking back at the ground already covered, but, instead, moving forward deliberately. According to Paul's example, we should concentrate our energies on moving forward into the future.

Where are you putting your focus? Have your goal in view—and keep your eyes, your heart, and your life fixed on the end of the race. We conquer by continuing…so press on!

Father, thank You for forgiving me and taking care of my past…and my future! Help me look ahead to see how I can serve You and run the course You've set before me. Amen.

God's Peace and Joy

❋

Do you struggle with depression? With negative thoughts? God promises you joy. No matter what your circumstances, you can have joy in Him. Philippians 4:4 says, "Rejoice in the Lord always. Again I will say, rejoice!" Rejoicing is not an option. And the truth is that the kind of rejoicing the Bible talks about often comes from a life of pain and hardship. But God's peace and joy will prevail. Philippians 4:6-7 says, "Be anxious for nothing, but in everything by prayer and supplication, with thanksgiving, let your requests be made known to God; and the peace of God, which surpasses all understanding, will guard your hearts and minds through Christ Jesus." God's peace stands guard against all those things that attack your mind and heart. Through prayer you'll also experience the joy God gives—His joy—in abundance (John 17:13-14).

Father, You are an awesome God! You not only give me the strength and fortitude I need to make it through my trials, but You also shower me with Your joy and peace along the way. Thank You! Amen.

The Flawless Word of God

❧

How gullible are you? I'm not asking in a derogatory or put-down way. I tend to believe what I hear, read, and watch. If you're like me, you realize there's definitely a need to discern truth. And that ability comes from learning, growing, and understanding the Bible. You may want to get involved in a Bible study or take some classes to further your knowledge. Memorizing Scripture is crucial to being able to separate fact from fiction. The American Banking Association once sponsored a training program to help tellers detect counterfeit bills. Not once during the training were the tellers exposed to actual counterfeits. For two weeks they handled nothing but the real thing. They became so familiar with the "true" that they couldn't be fooled by the false. And that's exactly what I'm encouraging you to do!

Jesus, memorizing takes time and energy, which are in short supply in my life. Please give me an energy boost and open my mind to Your Word. I want to do everything I can to know truth and learn about You! Amen.

Second Fiddle

❧

An interviewer asked famed conductor Leonard Bernstein, "What's the most difficult instrument to play?" Good-naturedly he replied, "Second fiddle!" He added, "And if no one plays second, there's no harmony." We need to be more than willing to be God's servants. We need to revel in the opportunities He gives us to serve.

Do you have someone you work with, serve with shoulder to shoulder? A woman you help as she serves the Lord? The apostle Paul said of Timothy in Philippians 2, "But I trust in the Lord Jesus to send Timothy to you shortly.... I have no one like-minded, who will sincerely care for your state" (verses 19-20). I pray that you'll spend time with a mentor in ministry and in prayer and Bible study. I encourage you to mature in your usefulness. Be content to play "second fiddle."

Jesus, You were so humble and willing to serve. I want to follow Your example. Keep me from being caught up in wanting to be in charge of everything. Help me look for places to serve and uplift others. Amen.

God's Dress Code

❊

"Hey if you're working out and 'lookin' good,' why not show it off?" That's a great question! And I've got a copy of God's "dress code" sitting right here in front of me. It's found in 1 Timothy 2:9, and it couldn't be clearer, "I also want women to dress modestly, with decency and propriety, not with braided hair or gold or pearls or expensive clothes, but with good deeds, appropriate for women who profess to worship God" (NIV). "Modesty." "Propriety." These two words are rare these days…both in speech and in media. If you profess godliness, your actions and your appearance should reflect your values. Good works are a great adornment for women who love God.

Jesus, I don't want to be old-fashioned, but I do want to please You. Give me discernment in how to dress so I represent You well. Thank You for Your free gift of salvation. Help me see opportunities to do good so people will be encouraged to seek You. Amen.

The Fickleness of Praise

❀

Faithfulness is a high calling. And you and I will have our reward if we serve well. So hang in there while doing good deeds and serving others. We're in this Christian life for the long haul. Yes, it's nice to be recognized for what we do, but that's not always going to happen. Our focus is on serving as representatives of Christ, sharing His love and concern and provision, not personal recognition.

As women we're in unique positions to reflect the softer, gentler side of faith in the Lord. We can show how kind and generous hearts, tempered by wisdom and strength, come from God. As we serve, we reflect His unconditional love. What an awesome privilege!

When all is said and done, one of our rewards may be praise, but the greater reward is being faithful to follow our Lord and Savior, Jesus Christ.

Lord, my ego likes it when people praise me for something I've done. Remind me always to give You credit. My gifts and the abilities to love and help others come directly from You. Amen.

Love the Sinner

A loving heart attitude is at the core of caring for others. When a friend sins, it's okay to hate her sin—in fact, that's a biblical principle. But we're to continue to love the sinner unconditionally. We are not to rejoice in another person's suffering or downfall, being glad that she "got what was coming to her." Jesus said in Matthew 12:34, "Out of the abundance of the heart the mouth speaks." Here's a little checkup you won't find in your doctor's office, but it could go a long way in keeping you spiritually healthy. John 13:34 says, "Love one another." Ephesians 6:18 says to pray for one another. Philippians 2:3 encourages us to respect one another. First Thessalonians 5:11 says to comfort and "edify one another." How's your heart? Are you living these biblical mandates?

Father, it's so natural to be petty, to be glad when someone who seems high-and-mighty is brought low. But that's not Your way. That's not how You love. I want to love unconditionally and purely like You. Show me how. Amen.

Parents, In-Laws, and You

❧

Today I want to go beyond the "God calls you to love" admonition and have a heart-to-heart with you about your parents and in-laws. Jim and I decided long ago that our parents were high priorities. We purposed to do everything we could for them. While they were younger, this didn't involve much. We visited regularly and kept in touch. As they got older, their challenges were greater, and we had many chances to serve. When Jim's mother's health failed, we willingly spent our time and resources to help her. When she died we had no regrets because we'd been there for her. The same applies to my father. And again as we, along with my siblings, watched out for my mother. Caring for our parents takes time, yes, and it takes money and effort. But it's well worth it…and pleases God!

Father, it's such a privilege to serve You. And I'm glad You've given me my parents and in-laws to love. Help me be patient, kind, and generous with my time and resources. Amen.

Pray for Your Children

❀

Praying for your children is the most powerful way you can care for them. Most times your heart will naturally overflow in prayer for them. And even when they're causing trouble or your patience is wearing thin, a quick prayer will calm your nerves and soothe your children. You'll be amazed at the huge difference prayer will make in the lives of your little ones. Ask God to show you how to let them know that after Him and your husband, they're more important than all the other people in your life.

Be ready to show your love. Set aside time each day to pray for your kiddos. And don't forget to pray for them when they're around. That lets them know you and God love them. It also helps them feel more secure and models prayer.

Praying for your kids is some of the best time you'll ever invest. Prayer is a powerful privilege!

Jesus, protect these little lives You've placed in my care. Help me be patient, calm, loving, and support- ive. Open their hearts to You. Amen.

32

A New Woman

❧

I'm sure you've been in grocery stores, libraries, and even parks where the kids were really wild. They don't listen to their parents and generally create havoc. I can relate to the parents of those unruly kids. Raising children didn't come easily for me, and in the early days of my marriage our home was chaotic. Thankfully Jesus came into our lives! When we became a Christian family, our girls were almost two and three years old. God—and His wonderful Word—came to our aid with practical guidelines for raising kids and creating a loving home. My life, my marriage, and my home were transformed as Jim and I, and eventually our girls, grew spiritually. I encourage you to use your Bible's index or get a concordance and search out the keys to a calm, loving home. Also talk with seasoned moms. You and your family will reap the rewards!

Father, I'm totally awed by what You've accomplished in my life. Your guidance and wisdom have made such a difference! I don't even want to imagine what life would be like without You. I praise Your holy name! Amen.

Love Your Home

❦

Are you tired of doing dishes, sweeping and vacuuming floors, dusting, picking up after other people? I can so relate. But it is worth it! Or at least it can be. You and I know that love is the world's most powerful motivator. So love your home—love being there and love managing it, watching over it, keeping it, and, yes, cleaning up the mess. Love will enable you and empower you to tackle it, master it, and excel at it. Turn to the Lord to fire up your passion in your heart to manage your home His way…in a loving, serving, sacrificial capacity. No task will be too difficult and no job will be meaningless with Him as the foundation.

Heavenly Father, sometimes I get tired of the mundane aspects of being a woman, wife, and mom. But I love You, my family, and my home. Help me find meaning in the little things that keep my life on Your path. Amen.

When You're Overwhelmed

❦

So many women I talk to feel overwhelmed. With responsibilities at school, church, home, and on the job there's just too much to do. I've probably just described your life, haven't I? Believe me, doing all that and trying to fit in Bible studies and worship and other activities related to being a Christian is no easy task. But you know what? The Old Testament shows us the way through Abraham. The Bible says he responded immediately to the call of God (Genesis 12:1-4; Hebrews 11:8). He trusted the Lord, and he moved out in obedience. What an encouragement to us! Whether the task at hand seems doable or not, the miracle of God occurs after we act in faith. Decide to do what God is asking of you in faith. That's when you'll truly know His provision!

Heavenly Father, today I'm going to step out in faith and willingly and joyfully do all I feel You are calling me to do. I know You'll give me the strength and time. Thank You. Amen.

I Shall Not Want

When is your church's next retreat? How long until your Bible study group gets together for fellowship? Do you catch an occasional radio broadcast or do quick devotional readings once in a while? Too often we neglect nurturing our spiritual lives by getting by on quick fixes. If your desire is to grow spiritually, you'll need to spend quality time in God's Word and more time in prayer.

I love Psalm 23, which starts, "The LORD is my shepherd; I shall not want." This so reminds me of my need for Him. Are you following the Shepherd? "He makes me to lie down in green pastures; He leads me beside the still waters. He restores my soul; He leads me in the paths of righteousness for His name's sake" (verses 2 and 3). Are you lying down in green pastures as the verse says? Are you feeding to your heart's content on His provision?

Father, You are my Shepherd. I want to follow You all of my days on earth...and into eternity. Restore my soul and refresh my spirit today. Amen.

Where He Leads

❧

What would you do if God suddenly called you to a different ministry? Sometime when you have a few minutes for yourself, take a card and write these words: *anything, anywhere, anytime, at any cost.* Then date the note. Can you in all honesty sign it? God's role is to lead us. Our job is to follow.

How are you doing? Have you looked into God's wonderful face and into His eyes of love and whispered, "Truly, dear Lord, where You lead me, I will follow"? Do these words express the deep longing of your heart? Are you following Him today? If not, will you?

> *God, You are my reason for living, my salvation, my comfort, my provider, my love. I choose today to follow You every step of the way. When the way gets hard and I falter, encourage me and give me strength. Amen.*

Meek to Mighty

❧

"I used to be so confident. But now I feel like such a loser." Do you feel this way? My friend, God never asks for us to have confidence. He only asks that we have confidence in Him! And when God commands, He also supplies. This is true for every area of your life.

In Old Testament times, the Midianites periodically destroyed the crops of the children of Israel. A young man named Gideon secretly "threshed wheat in the winepress, in order to hide it from the Midianites" (Judges 6:11). He doesn't sound very brave, does he? And yet we learn that God enabled and strengthened the meek Gideon into a mighty warrior, a man of valor, a man of mighty faith (Hebrews 11:32-33).

God will transform you too. Yield to Him. Trust Him. Allow Him to do great things in and through and for you.

Father God, when I'm hesitant to show faith in You, give me courage and the right words to say that will lead people to You. Open doors for me to bravely serve You and share Your truths. Amen.

The Strength to Go On

❧

Some hardships in life are devastating. The death of a husband, child, or parent, divorce, disappointment, betrayal…all are very difficult situations. How do you go on when tragedy strikes? How do you handle what life throws at you? The good news is that God will come to the rescue. His tender care goes into action with His promise to heal us. I love these four words in Psalm 23:3 that speak to my heart: "He restores my soul." Our wonderful Lord not only takes care of our physical needs, He also takes care of our spiritual needs. Isn't that uplifting? You can have hope in whatever your situation because He is a mighty and compassionate and loving God who will restore your soul. Hallelujah!

Father God, there's so much pain and suffering in this world…and I feel it too. It's hard to understand why life has to be so hard, but I'm so thankful I know You. You give me the strength to endure and still praise You. Amen.

39

A Model for the Home

❧

The woman of Proverbs 31 is a great model for home management. She does her husband good. She makes household items for her family and to sell. She shops wisely. She's very industrious. She buys land, plants crops, and invests. She keeps herself fit. This woman helps the needy. She's honorable, wise, and kind. She looks forward to the future. And her children and husband sing her praises. And no wonder!

Look to this amazing woman for inspiration. With God's help, you too can accomplish much. He calls you to tend your home and serve your family, and you do that in so many ways. But are you doing the best you can do? I encourage you to master new skills, express your creativity, and find new ways to help. Even if you work outside your home, you can make your home even better than "home sweet home." What an awesome privilege!

Father, thank You for blessing me with a home and for family and friends that fill it. Help me be industrious and cheerful as I encourage and serve everyone who comes in. Amen.

A Faithful Steward

❧

From basic necessities to cars, from supporting causes to vacations, the way we handle money reveals a lot. What has God entrusted to you? Do you have food in your cupboards and decent clothes for the family? Are you able to buy some luxuries, such as jewelry and going out to dinner? Financial responsibility is part of what God calls you to. The issue isn't how much or how little wealth you have, but how faithful a steward you are of what He has given you. First John 2:15 says, "Do not love the world or the things in the world."

I encourage you to do a Bible study on the numerous scriptures that give wise advice on handling money…and put into practice what you learn. As you live for the Lord's purposes and by His principles you'll find contentment.

Father, show me how You want me to spend my money. Open my eyes to the needs of people You want me to help. I want to find the right balance between providing for my family and helping others. Amen.

A Generous Soul

❊

Are you nurturing a giving spirit? Are you generous with all your resources? Giving God and people your time is sometimes the most expensive...and most appreciated...gift you can bestow. Generosity also includes little touches and activities you can do to brighten someone's day, such as sending a quick note, making a cheery phone call, weeding someone's flower bed, and delivering a bouquet of wildflowers.

I remember clearly the day I assessed my spiritual life and decided I needed help in this area. So I prayed...and continue to do so. Every day I ask God to open my eyes and my heart and to bring to my knowledge the needs of others. I consider it fine-tuning my heart to God's Word, God's ways, and God's grace. With His help I can meet the needs of others and reach out with His love. Why not make this one of your goals?

Father, show me the big and little ways I can share my resources, including my time. Help me think of others before myself when I have free time and some spending money. Amen.

The Right Path

❀

"Just relax. Go with the flow." We definitely live in a time that honors looseness. But that's not necessarily what being a woman after God's own heart is all about. We're to be the righteous saints of a righteous God. That doesn't mean we're perfect, mind you, but we are righteous in Christ: "By one Man's obedience many will be made righteous" (Romans 5:19). This means we're to be honorable, trustworthy, and follow God's precepts, even if that means running counter to the "easy" way, the "popular" way, the "don't get uptight" way.

God wants us to walk His paths. And He tells us in His Word how to do so. He also clearly spells out what He considers right and wrong. How blessed we are to have a God who cares for us and guides us!

Jesus, give me the courage to stand up for You and what You say is right. Remind me that You are my Guide so I don't get caught up in something or choose to ignore a situation that doesn't honor You. Amen.

Praise God!

❧

I'm so glad you're God's friend, that you have the promise of His blessings in your life. In Psalm 16:1, David says of God, "You will show me the path of life; in Your presence is fullness of joy; at Your right hand are pleasures forevermore." God will never fail you or change His mind about you. In His loving care you have a shelter in the storm and a haven when life bats you around. In His loving care you can have a generous heart because He provides abundantly. Use Psalm 23:6 as an affirmation of what you know to be true: "Surely goodness and mercy shall follow me all the days of my life; and I will dwell in the house of the Lord forever." Praise His holy name!

Jesus, I praise You! You've given me many astounding gifts and provided for and watched over me in countless ways. You are so wonderful, so powerful, so mighty, and so everlasting. And You love me. Amazing. Amen.

A Heart for Hospitality

❧

"I'm the kind of gal who has a refrigerator filled with bottled water, a few pieces of fruit, and a Diet Pepsi. Entertain? I don't think so!"

Are you like my friend? I'm hoping you'll reconsider! There are so many people around you who need love, friendship, support, and a relaxing time. Begin nurturing relationships by cultivating the art of hospitality (Romans 12:13). Then open your heart and home to others. And don't worry if your home isn't perfect. As long as it's tidy, you're good to go! Pick a time, invite guests, plan a meal or tasty snacks. Involve your family and prepare in advance to lessen stress. Pray about your gathering and then follow through. And most of all, be flexible and have fun! Your guests will be blessed...and so will you.

Jesus, I'm excited about this idea! Guide me in the next week or two as I think about who to invite, when to have the gathering, and what I need to do to prepare. Help me stay focused and not get overwhelmed. Amen.

Managing Money

✿

When it comes to finances, ignorance is not bliss. If you're married, do you and your husband share financial information? Are you both aware of income and expenses, home upkeep, taxes owed, and such? If you're single, do you track what comes in and what goes out? How can you hope to manage your finances if you don't know what you've got? Managing money, like any other discipline, starts with daily knowledge of your financial condition. We can't be casual about this matter of money because it's not ours! The money is God's. And if you're going to be someone who abounds in the grace of giving (2 Corinthians 8:3-7), you need to know your resources. It's a measure of your spiritual maturity. It's a discipline that makes you the woman you want to be.

Father, thank You for blessing me with what I need. Give me wisdom to carefully manage the resources You've given me so I can use it to provide for the people I care about and the causes You put on my heart. Amen.

Trust Him Fully

❧

"How can she be so mean? What did I ever do to her?" If you're facing this situation right now, I'm so sorry. Unfortunately, we're going to have difficult relationships all our lives, especially with those who don't know Christ. That's the nature of the fallen world we live in. But our hope and strength lie in Christ!

I have a question for you: If God is on your side, does it matter who is against you? Please don't mistake this for a lack of caring or understanding. I know it's not easy to be attacked. One thing I do for encouragement is turn to great hymns. In "Like a River Glorious," by Frances R. Havergal, the words are so appropriate: "We may trust Him fully all for us to do. They who trust Him wholly find Him wholly true." Trust Him, dear friend. He will comfort and protect you.

Father, relationships can be so hard and my feelings get easily hurt. Help me respond to negativity with Your grace and mercy. Comfort me with Your love. Amen.

Be Bold!

❀

People should never doubt where our faith lies. We're not secret agents. No way! Along with our friendliness and genuine concern and caring actions, we're to be bold. We're to be outspoken about our faith in Jesus Christ. And we should faithfully pray for opportunities to introduce our friends to the Savior. There's no greater gift than sharing the salvation offered through Jesus. It was the apostle Paul's desire "that God would open to us a door for the word, to speak the mystery of Christ" (Colossians 4:3). Paul wanted to declare Christ openly and to as many people as possible.

I encourage you to study God's Word and meet with other Christians so you can be prepared for questions people may have regarding Jesus. You don't have to know everything, but be comfortable with a few facts about your faith in Him. Then reach out with the true gospel!

Father, I want other people to experience Your love and have Your promise of eternal life through Christ. Show me people I can minister to, help me be prepared, and give me the words to speak. Amen.

Set Life Goals

❧

Is setting goals a challenge for you? Try it! God's servant Paul had goals. He tells us in Philippians that he was energized to "press on" to gain God's prize (Philippians 3:14 NASB). Setting goals will help turn your dreams into realities.

Several years ago Jim and I wrote out lifetime goals we believed would place God and His priorities at the center of our lives. And would you believe it? We're still following those goals! Why don't you jot down some ideas and mull over your gifts, your priorities, your lifestyle. Ask God for His wisdom and direction. Seek input from mentors and those closest to you. Then formulate some goals and set out on your life journey. And remember, your goals will adjust over time. Just keep your eyes and heart on Jesus for continual guidance.

Father, setting goals is intimidating. But I know they'll help me stay focused and be more effective in serving You. Give me Your wisdom and guidance as I set my goals…and help me carry them out. Amen.

Your Spiritual Gifts

❈

One of the best ways to discover your gifts is to ask God. When you're in the Word, for example, the Holy Spirit will show you ideas for service and ministry. People will come to mind, as will ideas for how to minister to them. I know a woman who's actively building a "Barnabas ministry" based on Acts 4:36. It's a ministry designed to encourage people who are suffering and need support by linking them up with others who have walked through their trials. Another friend operates what I call "Judy's Soup Kitchen." A nurse and cancer survivor, Judy knows just what's needed when someone's ill. So off she goes with her warm ways, her warm soup, and a batch of encouraging scriptures. Faithfully read your Bible and start developing your gifts!

Heavenly Father, You've given me gifts so I can serve Your people and encourage them in Jesus. Open my eyes to what You've given me and show me how to use them for Your glory. Amen.

Why Seek Peace?

❦

"What I need is rest. About a hundred years ought to about do it!" Don't we all feel this way at times! If I asked you to fill out a survey with one of the questions being, "What causes you to seek peace?" how would you answer? I responded to this question quickly: busyness. It's #1 on my list. There's always just "one more" of something to do. Responsibility is next. Tension is on the list too. Stress drains my energy. I'm sure you have your own list of feelings and activities and issues that make you crave peace. Here's the good news! Psalm 23:2 says, "[God] leads me beside the still waters." "Still waters!" Can't you just feel it? God knows your need for peace and He provides it. He ensures the restoration and calm you need to continue fulfilling His will for your life.

Father, replace my stress with Your peace and contentment. Renew in me the joy of life and service to You and those around me. Amen.

Be Generous

I vividly recall the day I began praying to be more generous. After assessing my spiritual life, I discovered I could use improvement in this area. So every day I ask God for opportunities to give. I pray for open eyes and an open heart that will recognize the needs of others. And God began to fine-tune my senses. Jim and I have been blessed to minister to many people through teaching, speaking, and writing. We also love to privately and quietly assist when we can.

The amazing results are that people have heard the Good News of Jesus Christ, people have been helped, and some people have accepted Christ as their Savior! On top of those wonderful blessings, the Lord has honored our commitment to Him in countless ways.

I encourage you to be generous with your gifts, your time, and your faith. And watch what God does through you!

Father, You've blessed me so much. As I share with others, keep my ego in check so that You get the recognition and thanks. Amen.

52

Experience God's Peace

❧

God provides real peace for us…and that includes you—even if you have a screaming baby, a high-stress job, or are knee-deep in troubles. You may not be feeling much like a woman after God's own heart, but John 16:33 records Jesus saying that even though in this world you will have tribulation, you also have God's perfect peace in every circumstance of your life. So even if at this moment you aren't able to fully appreciate the truth of God's peace, it's there and it will make itself apparent. First Corinthians 15:58 says, "Be steadfast, immovable, always abounding in the work of the Lord, [and here's the part for you today] knowing that your labor is not in vain in the Lord."

Bless you today and hang in there!

Father, thank You for caring so much about me that You know I need peace and rest. Restore my energy and my commitment to You and Your plan for my life. Amen.

A Positive Attitude

❧

It may surprise you to know that a positive attitude and the giving of thanks is willful…a choice you make. Giving thanks is a conscious decision, and it's also commanded by God. His Word tells us to give thanks always and for all things, in everything and evermore. First Thessalonians 5:16-18 says, "Rejoice always, pray without ceasing, in everything give thanks; for this is the will of God in Christ Jesus for you." That's pretty clear!

And the decision to do just that—to give thanks… no matter what…in whatever situation—has a powerful effect on your attitude. Not only that, it also has a huge impact on everyone around you. Philippians 4:7 says the peace of God that surpasses all understanding is available to you and me. Now that's something to be thankful for!

Father, even though You've blessed me so much, I still get stuck on what's not going right and the trials I face. Gently remind me that You're always with me. I want to maintain a thankful heart toward You! Amen.

Share Your Love!

❖

This is the perfect time to tell your husband, your children, your mom, dad, sisters, brothers, and your best friends how much you love them. What's so special about today? Nothing in particular…any day is a great day to let those closest to you know how much you love them! Also encourage them spiritually. Tell them you care how they feel and what they believe. And ask God to bless your loved ones and draw them closer to Him.

I have an idea! Make a list of those who matter most to you and tell each one how much you appreciate them. Write each person's name on different days on your calendar and on that day give them a call, write a note, send an e-mail card, deliver a small gift… your options are limited only by your imagination. Have fun as you bless the special people God brings into your life!

Father, in my busy days I forget to let people know how much I love them. Thank You for bringing them into my life. Bless them and watch over them. Amen.

Start with God

Do you wonder what to pray about or how to get started? I have a few suggestions that may help you. Start with God first: "Lord, thank You for loving me. I look around in amazement at Your lovely creation. Thank You for Your sacrifice so I can know You." Consider your relationship with Him: "Lord, what can I do today to live out the fact You are my ultimate priority?" Write down God's answers and promptings. Then ask, "Lord, what can I do today to grow spiritually? How can I prepare for future ministry?" Finish with, "Lord, what else would You have me do today?"

These simple prayers put your heart and feet in line with God and His plan.

Father, I love that I can come to You in praise... and get my questions answered. It amazes me that You care about the big and little things that happen in my life. I know You love me. Help me get over any awkwardness I feel about approaching You. Amen.

Good News!

❧

Do you know Jesus? Is He your Lord and Savior? Romans 3:23 reveals that we all have sinned. We all fall short of God's glory. And the penalty for sin is death…spiritual death. The Good News is Christ died for you (and me)! Romans 10:9 says, "If you confess with your mouth the Lord Jesus and believe in your heart that God has raised Him from the dead, you will be saved." Please take this opportunity to give your life to Jesus. Open yourself to His love and truth. Ask Him to come into your heart and be with you forever. He's waiting for you!

And if you already know Jesus, praise His holy name!

Jesus, I yearn to experience Your love. In my sin-filled heart I don't even come close to being as You are. Thank You for coming to earth and paying the price for my sins so I can know You personally. I accept Your free gift of salvation. Help me grow in You every day. Amen.

Watch, Listen, Act

✿

There's no better time than the present to notice other people's needs and do something about them. Yes, even during your busiest times. Proverbs 20:12 says, "The hearing ear and the seeing eye, the LORD has made both of them." Be watching and listening to those around you. That's exactly what God does in our lives. He watches and listens and responds in loving care for our every need. Follow Dorcas' example. She was a woman "full of good works and charitable deeds which she did" (Acts 9:36). This thoughtful lady noticed the widows needed clothes, and so she acted on it and made some for them. Ask God to lead you to people who need encouragement, support, and prayer. Notice those around you and keep a keen eye out for ways you can actively help.

Jesus, surely You set up divine appointments every day so I can be used by You to meet a need. Help me watch and listen for those opportunities to say a kind word or do a charitable deed. May others see Your goodness in my outstretched hands. Amen.

58

Prayer Will Change Your Life

✦

Do you have trouble praying? Are you uncertain whether it accomplishes anything? Let me assure you that prayer can change your life in ways you've never imagined. Why do I encourage you to pray? For one thing, I don't want you to miss out on a ton of blessings! Prayer increases your faith in God and eases your burdens. It opens your heart to His love and peace and encouragement on those days full of panic and stress. Prayer also changes lives—yours and the people you pray for. Prayer helps you focus on others and not yourself, which usually improves relationships. Prayer brings contentment as you commune with God. It opens the path to God's wisdom so you can be confident in making decisions. And prayer is a powerful ministry. James 4:8 says, "Draw near to God and He will draw near to you."

Father, I lift my voice and praise to You. Help me know that You're listening. Give me Your strength and wisdom today. Draw close to me. Amen.

About the Author

❦

Elizabeth George is a bestselling author and national speaker who is dedicated to helping people live a life after God's own heart.

Women around the world are drawn to Elizabeth's approach of daily starting with the Bible to handle life's challenges. Her ability to weave biblical truth into everyday issues has led readers to make more than 15 of her books bestsellers. Elizabeth's distinctive work, *A Woman After God's Own Heart*, remains a treasured gift for moms and grandmothers and made the CBA Bestseller List for 14 consecutive months.

Elizabeth also encourages women through her radio broadcast, *A Minute for Busy Women*, featured on Christian radio stations across America and at www.OnePlace.com. She is also a regular keynote speaker at women's conferences and retreats.

Elizabeth and her husband, Jim, are parents and grandparents and have been active in ministry for more than 30 years.

www.elizabethgeorge.com
Facebook:www.facebook.com/pages/Elizabeth-George
Twitter: @elizabethupdate